My
BEST
DAY I

A collection of best day remembrances of celebrities,
athletes and other prominent Americans
MARK KEYS

M K
C E
C Y
O S
O
L
PRESS

No part of this publication may be reproduced, distributed, or transmitted in any form by any means, including photocopying, recording, or other electronic or mechanical methods, or by any information storage and retrieval system, without prior written permission from the publisher, except for brief quotations embodied in critical reviews and certain other noncommercial uses permitted by copyright law. For permission requests, write to the publisher, addressed

McCool Keys Press
5308 Neptune
Newport Beach, CA 92663

Individual Sales, This book is available through most bookstores or can be ordered directly from McCool Keys Press at the address above.

Quantity Sales. Special discounts are available on quantity purchases by corporations, associations, and others. For details, contact the "Special Sales Department" at the publisher's address above.

Printed in the United States of America.

Library of Congress Cataloging-in-Publication Data is available from the publisher.

ISBN 978-0-9897878-4-0

Cover Design Concept by Mark Keys & Kendall Roderick

Cover design and text design by Kendall Roderick (RMind-Design.com)

The text for this book is set in Century

Dedication

For Laurie, Page, Megan, Mom and Dad.

For my entire extended family:
Dr. Michael Gordon, Tyler Mimm and their staff;
Chuck Bailey, the Moores, Marchoskys, Frank & Connie
Clark, Blain Skinner, Chris Clark & family, Joe & Roberta
McCarthy and the entire McCarthy Family.

For all my other family members and friends who have supported me throughout my recent years of rehabilitation and while preparing this book.

In memory of Shelly Savage Larson,
daughter of the late David Swede Savage.

FORWARD:

Bravery can be physical and obvious or it can be something much more subtle—but nonetheless heroic in its manifestation.

Everyday Mark Keys does something brave, beginning with the simple act of rising from his bed. No easy task for a person whose body bristles with the mostly unseen residue of several back injuries. Telltale scars inside and out, fused bones, exotic metals, and constant pain, are his battlefield. Yet, without fail, Mark cares for his family in a seemingly effortless way that stems from his deep core of courage. His wife and young daughters know that no matter what he will always be there for them as a husband and father.

Now, Mark has a family of friends. They are all happily here in My Best Day because Mark's heartfelt letters of interest touched them, his enthusiasm captivated them, and his bravery won their hearts—as it has mine.

— LT. COL. CHUCK BAILEY
Pilot, United States Air Force (Retired)

INTRODUCTION

In May, 1991, I injured my back while working and was placed on permanent disability. Prior to my first back surgery, I had my photo taken with Magic Johnson of the Los Angeles Lakers. Later, Blain Skinner, a friend of mine, was able to get Magic to autograph the snapshot. It made my day.

As a hobby, I began writing to other celebrities asking for autographed photos. Their positive responses amazed me. One weekend while in Palm Springs, California, I met Nat Kipner, an entrepreneur, who suggested I expand my hobby to include famous people from all walks of life. This idea was a godsend. During the next several years, while incapacitated with several more back surgeries and an ankle reconstruction, I collected even more autographs.

One day while out walking, I notice the magnificent beauty of the simple blue sky. Upon returning home, I thought about what a good day it was, despite my back problems. I felt great! Then it struck me: I wondered what all those people I had been receiving autographs from felt was their "best day."

I began writing letters asking that question. Joey Bishop was the first to reply, and that's how it all began. After I collected hundreds of letters, I knew that my collection make an inspirational book. I hope you will agree.

My best day was when I saw the water from the Pacific Ocean splashing on the window of my spacecraft (Apollo 13). Then I knew I finally made it.

—JAMES LOVELL

NASA Astronaut/Navy commander, Apollo 13 lunar mission

. . . one day in the spring of 1961 when I heard from a rather small publishing house in New York that they would publish my book, Sex and the Single Girl . . . so many things came from the publication of the book—money, recognition, finally the beginning of Cosmopolitan, which has been my work and a huge part of my life for so many years.

— **HELEN GURLEY BROWN**

Author/Former
editor-in-chief, Cosmopolitan

. . . the day I successfully landed my Corsair fighter plane on the deck of a small carrier called the Guadalcanal (I was a Marine Corps Fighter Pilot in World War II). There have been others . . . the day I got my wings, the day I met Johnny Carson, and the day I met my beautiful wife Pam.

—ED MCMAHON

Actor/TV personality, Tonight Show, Star Search

Today is my best day.

—DEAN MARTIN

*Singer/Actor/Entertainer; The
Dean Martin Show, Oceans 11,
Martin & Lewis Movies,
Rio Bravo*

Getting the go-ahead for Damn Yankees, my first trip to Broadway . . . and the days ever since.

—JERRY LEWIS

Actor/Director/Producer; spokesman for Muscular Dystrophy Labor Day Telethon, Cinderfella, The Nutty Professor

I consider myself fortunate in having many "best" days in my life. However, on January 17, I received the Presidential Medal of Freedom at the White House. No one could claim to be equal to this honor but I will cherish it for as long as I live.

—BOB DOLE
Former U.S. Senator,
Presidential Nominee

. . . the day Mr. Ed spoke to me.

—ALAN YOUNG
Actor, Mister Ed, Time Machine,
The Alan Young Show

There is one particular day that will always stand out in my mind. The town I grew up in, Harvey, Illinois, named a street after me. This was so very meaningful to me because I grew up with eight brothers and sisters and we were truly the poorest family in Harvey. I shined shoes in taverns and sold newspapers on the corner. I set pins in bowling alleys and caddied in the summertime. So to . . . have a street named after me turned out to be quite a special day.

—TOM DREESEN
Comedian/Entertainer, The Rat Pack, Trouble with the Curve

On May 31, 1973, in the Indianapolis 500, lap thirty-three, Swede Savage realized his child-hood dream—to lead the Indy 500. However, only moments later his car would crash in to the wall coming out of turn four and that crash would eventually lead to his death thirty-three days later. In this case, it would have to be best day/worst day.

— DAVID SWEDE SAVAGE
Race Car Driver, shared by his widow, Sheryl

. . . the day my son came out of a coma after being unconscious for seven days.

—JOE PATERNO
Head Football Coach,
Penn State

. . . I have had two best days: the birth of my daughter, Carrie, and the birth of my son, Todd. They have been my greatest source of happiness throughout the years and I thank the good Lord every day for the blessings He has bestowed on me, through my children.

—DEBBIE REYNOLDS
Actress, The Unsinkable Molly Brown, Singing in the Rain, Halloweentown

The day I married my wife—fifty-six years ago. January 14, 1941.

—JOEY BISHOP
Comedian/Actor, The Joey Bishop Show, Oceans 11

The time the Lakers won the championship by defeating the Celtics on their own home floor—something which had never been done before . . . any father would always consider the birthday of one of his children as the best day in his life. This has happened to me six times, so I'm blessed with a week full of beautiful days.

—**JERRY BUSS**
Owner, Los Angeles Lakers

. . . the Sunday back in April, 1949, when Ann Estock and I decided to run off and get married, was the greatest single event to take place in my life. Ann was sixteen years old and I was nineteen. We slipped away in my dad's car and drove from Birmingham, Alabama to Risen Fawn, Georgia, to be married secretly. We were too young to know better, but we've been married forty-six years.

—BOBBY BOWDEN
Head Football Coach, Florida
State University

1. First ride into space, April 16, 1985.
2. When we realized we had really fixed the Hubble space telescope, New Year's Eve 1993.

—DR. JEFFREY A. HOFFMAN
NASA Astronaut

I have had five best days, each at the birth of a child, the last birth being twins. But the kind of day to which you must have referenced is the day I read the following bit of philosophy: "At the moment of commitment the entire universe conspires to assure your success."

— **NORMAN LEAR**

Producer, All in the Family, The Jeffersons; Sanford & Son

When I was a child of six months to the day she died, every day I looked into my mother's lovely face.

—RAY WALSTON
Actor, My Favorite Martian,
Picket Fences

The day I started The Lone Ranger TV shows.

—CLAYTON MOORE
Actor, Lone Ranger, The Adventures of Kit Carson

. . . July 19, 1996, the day I carried the U.S. flag into the Olympic Stadium, at the 1996 Olympics in Atlanta, Georgia . . . having 100,000 people cheering and screaming when I entered the stadium was a thrill and an honor—the biggest honor of my sporting career.

—BRUCE BAUMGARTNER
Four-Time Olympic Medalist; Wrestling

All my days have been good days, but some have had better results than others.

—GENE STALLINGS
Head Football Coach, University of Alabama

Carrying the flag for my Judo team in the 1964 Olympic parade was certainly inspirational. Representing my American Indian heritage by riding my horse in the 1993 Presidential Inaugural parade was most definitely a once-in-a-lifetime experience I will never forget. And the days I won seats in the U.S. Congress and the Senate were certainly unforgettable. However, in retrospect, my best day was, without a doubt, the day I met my wife, Linda.

—BEN NIGHTHORSE CAMPBELL
U.S. Senator

. . . the day my baby girl was born, because I had stated that I wanted a girl child and went to work with charts and thermometers to get her. She was born the morning of September 9, 1971.

—MORGAN FREEMAN

Actor, Driving Miss Daisy, The Shawshank Redemption, Seven, Bruce Almighty

When I met my last wife.

—PAT PAULSEN
Comedian/Actor, Laugh-In

It will come June 7th when my wife, Barbara, who has worked for many years, will graduate from the University of Utah. It will be very pleasing to me because I enjoy myself most when I see people who have worked very hard to get their just reward.

—FRANK LAYDEN
President/Former Head Coach,
Utah Jazz

My daughter, Jenna, fresh home from school, entered my den. "I need your help with my homework," she said.

"What is it?" I asked.

"We're supposed to write an essay about our favorite hero."

"Do you need a ride to the library?" I offered.

"No, I want to interview you."

—RICHARD PAUL EVANS
Author, The Christmas Box, The Locket, Timepiece

. . . the day Christian Slater's interview with People magazine came out, Christian, when asked . . . to choose a role model . . . chose me. Since I'm very close to Christian, that meant a lot to me. That same night Charles Durning and Peter Falk were at a play-reading I put together. I overheard my name being mentioned and Peter saying, "That Dan is a hell of an actor." Charles replied, "And a good guy." Love and respect from my peers, what more could I ask for in one day?

—DAN LAURIA
Actor, The Wonder Years, Independence Day, Sullivan & Son

My best day? I've had so many. Playing the Palace on Broadway in vaudeville with my sister Vilma in 1930 was certainly one. Opening in Flying Colors, a Broadway show, with Vilma was another. Winning the Trans Pac in my catamaran was certainly a best day. But, thinking back over the years, reviewing the paths I've traveled, and where I am today, my best day was the day I married Dorothy.

—BUDDY EBSEN
Actor, Beverly Hillbillies, Breakfast at Tiffanys, Barnaby Jones

. . . the day I am living right now because I can remember all the yesterdays and can look forward to all the tomorrows, and if the tomorrows do not come, at least I had my best day. (P.S. If you want to know my worst day, I have a lot of those.)

—SHECKY GREENE
Comedian/Actor, Combat

As a young aerial gunner on a B-24 Liberator during WWII, after coming back from Germany on my thirtieth and final mission—I kissed the ground and it was all over—I survived.

—CHUCK BEDNARIK
Hall of Fame Football Linebacker/Center, Philadelphia Eagles

I've been blessed with many good days in my personal and professional lives, more than I honestly deserve. But by far the best day of all must have been the day I married my wife, Fighting Heart Jean Grace Goebel Rather. All the other good days since then have only been made sweeter by her—and neither the days nor I would have amounted to anything without her.

—DAN RATHER
Anchor of CBS Evening News

I have to think of the time our children were born or when they were married or when we found out my wife did not have cancer . . . but the greatest day of my life would be when I decided to turn it over to Jesus Christ.

—LOU HOLTZ
*Head Coach, University of
Notre Dame*

All of 'em!!!

—ARTE JOHNSON
Comedian/Actor, Laugh-In,
Night Gallery

The day the hostages walked off the plane on American soil, which I covered for ABC News. The first shuttle launch, which I also covered. I'll never forget the emotions evident that day in Washington or the feel of the TV trailer vibrating because of the propulsion at lift-off.

—CHET FORTE
Director, ABC's Monday Night Football

. . . My first day of filming the Mission Impossible series. It was wonderful career and the people I worked with became my closest friends.

—PETER LUPUS

Actor, Mission Impossible, Police Squad!, Muscle Beach Squad

My best day is every new day. Once again I'll have the opportunity to contribute something to some-one, to be productive, and to love my wife.

—LYLE WAGGONER
Actor, Carol Burnett Show,
Wonder Woman

My best day is receiving this letter from you.

—BILL DAILY
*Actor, Bob Newhart Show, I
Dream of Jeanie*

. . . the birth of my son, Michael, even though I fainted at the circumcision. It was thrilling as Lucille Ball (his godmother) handed me this seven pounds of delight—who now towers over me at six feet, while I'm shrinking. Lovely, exciting day.

—JACK CARTER
Actor/Comedian; Cavalcade of Stars, Mr. Wonderful, The Joey Bishop Show

. . . the eve of the Riverside 500 in 1964. Seated at the head table of the pre-race dinner was my soul-mate, Shelby Grant—she was Queen of the Riverside 500. The moment I laid eyes on her I was, as the Italians say, "thunderstruck." We are approaching our thirtieth anniversary.

—CHAD EVERETT
Actor, Medical Center,
Mulholland Drive

Every day has the best day potential.

—**BONNIE HUNT**
Actress, Jerry Maguire, The
Bonnie Hunt Show, Cheaper
by the Dozen

When I got my first professional job, Burns & Allen . . . first movie, Seven Brides for Seven Brothers . . . first standing ovation . . . last standing ovation. When the Soviets let me bring my ninety-year-old grandmother to the U.S. from Siberia.

—RUTA LEE

Actress/TV personality; Seven Brides for Seven Brothers, Funny Face, Witness for the Prosecution

. . . the day my television series, Johnny Mann's Stand Up and Cheer, was successfully produced. Since it espoused God and country through music, I felt I had finally contributed something worthwhile to America.

—JOHNNY MANN
Recording Artist/TV Personality

. . . when I first headlined at the Flamingo Hotel in Las Vegas. After doing primarily comedy in my act for years, I decided to add a dramatic hunk (doing the final scene in Camelot as Richard Burton)! I was given a standing ovation—stopped my own show—and couldn't have been more thrilled. For one brief moment . . . I had my best day.

—FRANK GORSHIN

Actor/Impressionist, "The Riddler" in the Batman TV series

The day I was born. My mother once asked me on my birthday if I was glad I was born. It has never occurred to me not to be.

—DAVE BRUBECK
Jazz Musician

In 1963, I won the most valuable player award while pitching softball for the Negro Actors Guild in the Broadway show League.

—GEORGE C. SCOTT

Actor/Director, Patton, Dr. Strangelove, The Day of the Dolphin

. . . today. I can look at the past and be thankful for how much I've learned from others. And I can think about the future with renewed vigor because some beautiful people around me have given me hope that good will win out over evil.

—**VIC BRADEN**
Tennis Professional

. . . any day when I have my wife (of fifty-nine years), three children, seven grandchildren and eight great-grandchildren together with me at a dude ranch, beach house, or mountain retreat for a full three days.

—ART LINKLETTER
TV personality, Kids Say the Darndest Things

As an athlete: winning the World Championship with the New York Knickerbockers in 1970 and 1973. Legislative achievement: passage of the Tax Reform Act of 1986. I am proudest of fulfilling the role of father. Virtually nothing has given me more pleasure or my life more meaning.

—BILL BRADLEY

Former U.S. Senator, Professional Basketball Player; New York Knicks

The day was November 28, 1983, the time was 11:15AM EST. The place was the Kennedy Space Center, Florida. The occasion was the ninth launch of the space shuttle (STS-9), a mission called SpaceLab-1, on the orbiter Columbia and I was onboard! The next thing I knew, the launch tower was disappearing through the side window and we were on our way to orbit! Our final speed was just under 18,000 miles per hour, to put us in orbit about 150 miles above the surface of the earth.

—BYRON K. LICHT-ENBURG, SC.D.
NASA Astronaut

The birth of our first daughter was part of my most memorable day—that having been preceded by thirty-seven hours of labor, walking, pain and tears because my husband was in the army far away. She was a plump eight-pound, pink darling. That night my husband came to my hospital room at midnight or so. He had hitch-hiked in the rain from Camp Roberts. We talked and laughed. He kissed me and slipped his battered infantry ring on my finger. Then he said, "I'm AWOL. Have to get back, love." and he was gone. The next day everyone said I had merely dreamed his visit and only believed me when I showed them his ring.

—ROSEMARY DECAMP

Actress, That Girl, Bob Cummings Show, Yankee Doodle Dandy

. . . when my children were born.

—JACK KLUGMAN
*Actor, Odd Couple, Quincy,
M.E., 12 Angry Men*

My best day is today and my next best day
is tomorrow.

—LARRY HAGMAN
Actor, I Dream of Jeanie, Dal-
las, Primary Colors, The Group

My best day is today.

—WALTER MATTHAU

*Actor, Grumpy Old Men, Odd
Couple, Taking of Pelham 1-2-3*

Between my family life and my basketball, there have been too many to name. I am a fortunate man and I am thankful for that. I will leave you with an old Irish toast to the New Year . . .

"May your right hand always be reaching out for friendship and not in want."

—JIM CALHOUN
Head Basketball Coach, University of Connecticut

Any day I don't have a root canal is a good day.

—PHYLLIS DILLER
*Comedienne/Actress, Phyllis
Diller Show, A Bugs Life*

So far, it was July 3, 1947, in the sense I was born then. Everything that happened after that was pretty much inevitable.

—DAVE BARRY
Humorist/Columnist/Author

I'd have to say it was the night I fought my last fight—after having guys take whacks at you for eighteen years (that's how long I was a fighter), to say to the world "Good—that's enough" was a great thrill!

—ART ARAGON
Boxer, "The Golden Boy"

Certainly when all my children were born—my grandchildren and whenever the Dodgers won a game.

—BARRY SULLIVAN
Actor, Suspense, Framed; shared by daughter, Jenny Sullivan

On that day in my thirteenth year, I walked down the aisle; while the congregation sand an invitational hymn, confessed my faith in Jesus as the Son of God and my Savior, and was baptized . . . I experienced the most incredible feeling of my life! What could ever top that?

—PAT BOONE
Singer/Actor, April Love,
State Fair

A. My Wedding day.
B. My son's birth.

—JAYNE MEADOWS
Actress, I've Got a Secret; married to Steve Allen

. . . the day my son inducted me into the Pro Football Hall of Fame, on July 31, 1993, in Canton, Ohio. It meant a great deal to have my son by my side and be a part of that very special occasion. I felt emotions that no record or championship could ever bring.

—WALTER PAYTON
Hall of Fame Professional Football Player, Chicago Bears

Really haven't had a bad day. My best day is yet to come, and I enjoy looking and living for it every day—honest!

—HUGH O'BRIAN
Actor, Wyatt Earp; founder, chairman of development, acting president and CEO of Youth Foundation

. . . the day Nellie said "yes" and later "I do."

—JOHN WOODEN
Head Basketball Coach, UCLA,
"Wizard of Westwood"

. . . my years with Burns & Allen . . . my many sea-sons with Jack Benny . . . the fun I had with Fred MacMurray on My Three Sons . . .my twenty-two years with Johnny Carson . . . the very pleasant relationship I'm having now with Jay Leno. Let's just say that I've had a lot of good times.

—FRED DE CORDOVA
*Director/Producer, Burns &
Allen, Tonight Show*

. . . the day my son was born. I was there during the delivery, in Boone, North Carolina, and I'll always treasure that day. It's amazing watching someone come to life.

—BOBBY CREMINS

Head Basketball Coach, University of Georgia Tech

Career: I auditioned for Call Me Mister (1946) and got the job. Personal: My wife having our children, and being told wife and child were doing well.

— BUDDY HACKETT
Comedian/Actor, It's a Mad, Mad, Mad, Mad World, The Love Bug, The Little Mermaid

I've had several best days: the day I got married, the birth of my first son, Phillip—in fact, the birth of all my seven sons—and now the birth of my first grandson.

—JOSEPH CAMPENELLA
Actor, Ben, Hanger 18, The Fugitive

My wedding day and the days when my two children were born.

—GREG NORMAN

Professional Golfer, "The Great White Shark"

. . . in my athletic career, it was marching in the opening ceremonies of the 1964 Olympic Games in Tokyo, Japan, as a twenty-year-old representing the United States of America—my country. I was on the volleyball team and it was the first time I was on foreign soil. It was an experience I will never forget.

—KEITH ERICKSON

Player Phoenix Suns, LA
Lakers; Announcer LA Lakers,
LA Clippers

The day I was born . . . no cares! I'm still the happiest guy I ever met!

—MOREY AMSTERDAM
Actor/Comedian, Dick Van Dyke
Show, The Morey Amsterdam Show

. . . the day in 1945 when I stepped off an aircraft carrier in San Francisco. World War II was over for me and I had survived eighteen months of heavy combat against the Japanese.

—DEWEY MARTIN
*ctor, Big Sky, The Proud &
Profane, The Longest Day*

1. Got married to Kay.
2. Daughter Francesca born.
3. Son Jason born.
4. Daughter Hudson born.

—TOM POSTON
Actor, Bob Newhart Show, The Steve Allen Show

My most fortunate best day was September 9, 1961—the day I married my wife, Barbara. She has been the strength of our family and the person who has set the table for opportunities and successes in my life.

—BILLY PACKER
Sportscaster, CBS Sports

I cannot name one day, rather, after careful consideration I look back on three of the most thrilling, spiritual, mystical, beautiful and most productive days that stand out in my mind—the births of my three children. When number one arrived, this was the first time I had ever held a baby in my arms. Now a grown, handsome man, he is my rock of Gibraltar. Number two, a beautiful, brilliant, radiant daughter . . . a joy. And number three, the cute, funny, precious boy who captured everyone's heart. Three treasures . . . and the greatest days of my life.

—MARGARET BURK
Author/Co-Founder, Round Table West

. . . the day I arrived in New York, in 1946, en route to Hollywood and MGM. My contract was all signed and sealed, and I was about to appear in The Hucksters with Clark Gable . . . it was most exciting to be making my Hollywood debut with such a big star, at the tender age of twenty-five!

—DEBORAH KERR

Actress, An Affair to Remember, From Here to Eternity, The King and I

It would be difficult to decide in my roller coaster existence, just when I had my "best day."

Perhaps it was the day I married my present wife, Vera. Or the days when my three children were born.

Certainly the day I came away cancer-free from a prostate operation stands near the top. For now, everyday seems as if it should be the best day of them all.

—**ROBERT GOULET**
Actor/Singer, Beetlejuice, I deal in Danger, Toy Story II

Every day I do a game . . . it is the best! Awesome baby!

—DICK VITALE
Basketball Analyst/Author

. . . the day I was born, because I've had many, many special and wonderful days and consider myself a very fortunate person.

—LOIS NETTLETON
Actress, Centennial, Stars of
Jazz, Dr. Kildare

. . . when my three children and grandchildren (three) come over for holidays or Sundays and we have a love-in. We are an affectionate bunch and enjoy being together.

—MONTY HALL
TV host/personality,
Let's Make a Deal

When you've lived to be ninety-plus . . . it's almost impossible to single out one particular best day . . . Oh, of course the day I met Betty (my wife of sixty-two years); opening night at the Pasadena Playhouse; my first screen test . . . and when I got the contract . . . Maybe the best day of all was Christmas Eve when my brother and I hid on the upstairs landing and watched my dad bring a Flexible Flyer sled into the house . . . what a Christmas that was—snow and everything!

—ROBERT YOUNG

Actor, Marcus Welby,
M.D., Three Comrades,
Northwest Passage

Christmas, and all that it means.

—JUNE ALLYSON
*Actress, Little Women, Glenn
Miller Story, My Man Godfrey*

Every day is my best day.

—DYAN CANNON
*Actress, Heaven Can Wait, Bob
& Carol & Ted & Alice*

1. The day I was born to kind and loving parents.
2. The day I married my wonderful husband.
3. The day my marvelous children were born.
4. The day my interesting career started.

These things would have been impossible without the "Great One" upstairs, from whom all my blessings flowed.

—ELAINE STEWART
Actress, Brigadoon, The Bad & The Beautiful,

Being on stage making 1,500 people laugh their socks off!

—BERNARD FOX
Actor, Bewitched, The Mummy

The birth of my daughter was, by far, the very best day I can remember. Also, the day I opened in Top Banana, the musical show, with Phil Silvers, at the Wintergarden Theatre in New York and got a standing ovation when I walked on the stage (before I even said a word)!

—ROSE MARIE
Actress, Dick Van Dyke Show,
Psycho, Top Banana

. . . the birth of my son, Jamie MacDougall, who is now a dermatologist in Manhattan Beach, California. Of course, a best day to make this all possible was my wedding day to my darling late husband, Ranald MacDougal.

—**NANETTE FABRAY**
Actress/Singer, Our Gang comedies, Coach, Harper Valley PTA

. . . the day my National Actors Theatre finally came into being in 1991—it was truly the realization of my dream.

—TONY RANDALL
*Actor, Odd Couple; Pillow Talk,
Lover Come Back*

My best day was when you asked for my best day.

—ANTHONY CARUSO
Actor, To the Victor, Asphalt Jungle

The biggest thrill was my first Derby—Lauren-1938. I never thought I would win one. Not five.

—EDDIE ARCARO
Jockey, Five-Time Kentucky Derby Winner

. . . very definitely when Nan and I were married. She was the light of my life.

—FRANKIE LAINE
Singer/Songwriter/Actor, Raw-hide, High Noon

. . . twenty years ago with my family and friends, on Martha's Vineyard. A day of tennis, fishing and swimming—followed by spaghetti at Luigi's, fireworks in the sea-side park, and ending with a Hitchcock film!

—PETER BONERZ
Actor/Director, Bob Newhart
Show, Catch-22, The Bastard

. . . being called by King Features Syndicate to take over Blondie, back in 1984. What can I say? Who wouldn't have found that his best day?

—**STAN DRAKE**
Cartoonist, Blondie

My best days were when my babies were born and every day when I'm with my brothers and my family—and the day I was born in America.

—TONY LOBIANCO
Actor, The Juror, The French Connection

October 3, 1951. Giants/Dodgers playing for the pennant. Last of the ninth inning, Dodgers are winning 4-2. One out, two men on, I got up and hit the "shot heard round the world," to win the pennant 5-4.

—BOBBY THOMSON
Professional Baseball Player,
New York Giants

. . . my first day on my first Hollywood movie, filmed in New York, just a few blocks from where I lived. All the neighbors were curious to know what the kid from West 64th Street was doing walking with Humphrey Bogart.

—NEHEMIAH PERSOFF
Actor, Some Like It Hot, On The Water Front

The birth of my babies, my wedding day (days), my discovery, my first movie . . . my children being my friends.

—JANET LEIGH
Actress/Author, Psycho, The Naked Spur, Little Women

. . . the day I married my Kay, thirty-five years ago, as it put my life in the proper perspective. I had just returned from a world tour of entertaining our troops, in the All Army show—and as satisfying as the applause and laughter is, it certainly can't compare to home and family. Kay and I have been blessed by God, who has allowed us to share our youth, our middle years, and hopefully our later years together, knowing the joys of raising a terrific family.

— **RON MASAK**
*Actor, Murder She Wrote,
Second Effort*

The last race I rode.

—JOHNNY LONGDEN
Jockey, Triple Crown Winner

My best day was forty-three years ago when I was married. I have been happy ever since.

—DICK VAN PATTEN
Actor, Eight is Enough, Joe Kidd, High Anxiety

My The best? I guess the one film of mine with the fewest mistakes: *The Apartment.*

—BILLY WILDER
Screenwriter/Director/Producer,
Some Like It Hot

Every Sunday!

—GEORGE BLANDA
Professional Football Player,
Houston Oilers, Chicago Bears,
Oakland Raiders

1. First kiss.
2. First love.
3. First audience (that means me)!
4. Being shot at unsuccessfully.
5. Tennis, chess, or sailing victories.

—WILLIAM WINDOM
*Actor, Murder She Wrote, The
Detective, To Kill a Mockingbird*

. . . started when I woke up this morning, and tomorrow will be even better because I will make it better.

—JACK LALANNE
Fitness Expert/Author

. . . every day when I wake up . . . and am able to work.

—SIR JOHN GIELGUD

Author/Actor Julius Caesar, Arthur

. . . when I was playing Dr. Rank in Ibsen's The Doll House, with Queen Mary watching maybe fifteen feet away. She met me afterwards and was very gracious.

— **JOHN ABBOTT**
Actor, Deception, The Tempest, Mrs. Minerva

The day I got my own locker and major league
uniform with my name on it. It was a day my
prayers as a kid were heard.

—JOHNNY VANDERMEER
*Professional Baseball Player,
pitched back-to-back no-hitters,
Cincinnati Reds*

STS-80 (space shuttle) entry day, from de-orbit burn through roll out.

—STORY MUSGRAVE, M.D.

*NASA Astronaut, developed
SkyLab program*

. . . my first victory on the PGA tour . . . when you are paired with Nicklaus and Palmer in the last group and you beat them to win (Jackie Gleason Tournament, 1975). However, my best day is with my pals, my dad, my brothers, and my son-in-law. Wish we had more of the latter.

—BOB MURPHY
Professional Golfer

. . . in June of 1975, I went 5-6 with three home runs, one triple, one single and ten RBIs. The only out I made was a line out to second. We won 15-1.

—FRED LYNN
Professional Baseball Player,
Boston Red Sox

When you get to my age—every morning.

—REG SMYTH
Cartoonist, Andy Capp

I have never had a bad day. There is something good in every day. My best day would involve making someone else happy.

—GEORGE YARDLEY
*Hall of Fame, Professional
Basketball Player; Fort Wayne/
Detroit Pistons*

. . . when I joined the Cleveland Indians in 1946. Lou Boudreau signed me from an exhibition game against the Indians. In Cleveland Stadium, 80,000 people honored Babe Ruth, Ty Cobb and Tris Speaker—I had the honor that day of shaking hands with these immortals.

—**MAX PATKIN**
Clown Prince of Baseball

My best day was playing a Rose Kennedy-type on Roseanne. My best time was doing Sunshine Boys and Jose Ferrer.

—PHIL LEEDS
Actor; Rosemary's Baby,
Soap Dish

Everything became possible on my birthday.

—RUBY DEE
Actress, Jackie Robinson Story,
A Raisin in the Sun

You have asked a lucky man an easy question. My best day was the one in December when my beautiful mother gave birth to the adorable baby who has lived long enough to meet, marry, and enjoy life with a beautiful woman who, in turn, gave birth to our three beautiful daughters. All of those women, and our granddaughter, have provided me with three quarters of a century of best days.

—HAL KANTER
Director

My best day was May 18, 1972, when I met the Lord Jesus Christ as my Lord and Savior! Second best day: the day I married Anne, January 25, 1969.

—JIM RYUN
Member of the U.S. House of Representatives, U.S. Olympic team, 1964, 1968, 1972

My first ride at Indy. My wedding day. The day my son was born. The day my daughter was adopted. My first, second, and third Indy wins. I feel fortunate to have had so many.

—JOHNNY RUTHERFORD
Race Car Driver, Three Indianapolis 500 Wins

My best day? I've had so many, I'm the luckiest guy alive. I guess the best day was the day I was born when the good Lord handed me the gift of this wonderful life.

—ROBERT STACK
Actor; Eagle Squadron, Airplane!, Fighter Squadron, The Untouchables

You ain't livin' if you ain't laughin'.

—LESLIE NIELSEN
Actor, Naked Gun; Tammy &
The Bachelor, Harlow,
Naked Gun

The day my daughter Diane became the first Northern Cheyenne woman to graduate with an M.D. earning her degree from Stanford Medical School.

—**DOREEN "WALKING WOMAN" POND**
Author, Cheyenne Journey

Every day is my best day.

—RAY BRADBURY
Author; Martian Chronicles,
Fahrenheit 451

About the Author:

Mark Keys is a Southern California native, residing in Costa Mesa with his wife Laurie, daughters, Page and Megan, their dog, Fumble, and two cats, Lucy and Ethel. Mark loves that his mom still lives at the beach in Newport in the house he grew up in, and he spends a lot of time there with her & the girls; and loves walking the beach. He played basketball growing up, in High School, and beyond; as well as body surfed until he injured his back. Mark is an avid reader, enjoys watching classic movies & westerns, collecting film and sports memorabilia, walking and listening to Rat Pack music. He also loves to travel and going to sporting events, when health permits. In spite of his numerous surgeries, including 6 back, 9 ankle, 9 knee, and 2 shoulder surgeries, he also experienced shingles, pneumonia, MRSA Staph infection, he has no immune system and fights continuous headaches and other health issues every day. But, through all of this, he keeps a positive attitude and outlook to make each day, his best day.

Made in the USA
Monee, IL
13 May 2021

67416080R00075